T0208222

Evolution:

A Creative Journey to Inner Peace

Poetry and artwork by
Beth Noble

BALBOA
PRESS

Balboa Press books may be ordered through booksellers or by contacting:

Balboa Press
A Division of Hay House
1663 Liberty Drive
Bloomington, IN 47403
www.balboapress.com
1-(877) 407-4847

Because of the dynamic nature of the Internet, any Web addresses or links contained in
this book may have changed since publication and may no longer be valid. The views
expressed in this work are solely those of the author and do not necessarily reflect the
views of the publisher, and the publisher hereby disclaims any responsibility for them.

The author of this book does not dispense medical advice or prescribe the use of any
technique as a form of treatment for physical, emotional, or medical problems without the
advice of a physician, either directly or indirectly. The intent of the author is only to offer
information of a general nature to help you in your quest for emotional and spiritual well-
being. In the event you use any of the information in this book for yourself, which is your
constitutional right, the author and the publisher assume no responsibility for your actions.

ISBN: 978-1-4525-0031-7 (sc)
ISBN: 978-1-4525-0032-4 (e)

Library of Congress Control Number: 2010913966

Printed in the United States of America

Balboa Press rev. date: 02/03/2011

To the Indigo Girls, Byron Bay, Bungy and the Angels.

*Because in your own unique and perfect ways,
you showed me how to save myself.*

I'm not sure I would have made it without you.

Immeasurable thanks.

PREFACE

Almost two decades and many lifetimes ago, my life fell apart and I realised I did not have the inner resources to cope.

So I set out on a journey.

I stripped away layer after layer of who I'd been told I was, who I thought I should be or who I believed society wanted me to be.

The journey was inward. Driven by a profound longing to be Home. Not home in a physical sense, but rather in a deeply peaceful, remembering my true self sense.

And while I dabbled in almost everything available to 'New Age seekers', there was one constant, one tool that I kept coming back to, which was always there for me and has never ceased to give me the truthful answers and what I needed in that moment.

That gift was my creativity.

It opened the door for me to my deepest self. There I found sanctuary. There I found peace. There I came Home.

I wasn't qualified. I wasn't any good at first. I wasn't special. I was just desperate.

I tried it out and imagined myself to be a five year old so as not to judge what came.

It became my solace, my guidance, my friend, my confidante.

And I got lucky.

Over the course of some 15 years, I kept journals of the journey I was living through. The best (hopefully transpersonal) aspects of those words, scribbles, paintings and drawings have been distilled into this book.

The rest has been burned.

You can read this book from beginning to end. Or, if you wish, simply open to a random page and see what is the message for you in that moment.

For, as happens on the path to inner peace, this story does not always follow a clear and straight line.

While this is at once an intimate sharing of my experience, I hope it is not really about me and touches a place in you that helps you on your path. For while the road to inner peace is unique for each individual and sometimes impossible to speak of, let alone share, we need to be reminded that we are never truly alone.

So, I offer you *Evolution: A Creative Journey to Inner Peace*. With love, hope, joy, peace and freedom.

These are my wishes for you.

Evolution

First, there is the Call from deep within

The whisper

Of something else

Something more...

Followed by the Search

The hope

The promise

The struggle

The quest...

Then, with Grace,

The Rediscovery

The revelation

of the truth of who you really are...

Finally, living with this new awareness

This inner peace

When the world looks entirely different

Yet nothing has really changed.

The return Home

To Yourself.

The Journey to Wholeness.

A tiny seed lay deep within the rubble

Vulnerable
Damaged
Hungry

Waiting for life
To breathe its blessing

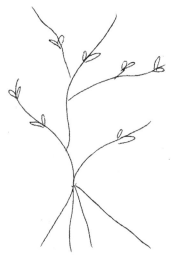

A tiny hand
Searched the ground
Prodding, poking
For something

Oblivious to the light it created

The seed saw the opening

The rain came

The journey began...

As it grew, weeds suffocated

Rubbish ignorantly thrown

The seed became thirsty for the rain

At times it lost sight of the sun

Hungry, beaten, hopeless

She was a simple soul
Searching for the elusive peace
She remembered from her youth
Beaten through years of pain
Tired, withered, lonely
Neglected her own garden, let overgrown
No time
She came to the rubble
Looking for a morsel of sustenance
Her parched fingers
Dug hungrily the earth

Her eye caught a glimpse
Green amidst the grey

Each day she came
Sharing what little she had

Both grew. Strong. Renewed.

And slowly

The doors began to open

      The rusty, creaking noise they made
      Was often loud and painful

         But as I started to see
         What was behind them

               My tiny, weak spirit

Began to unfold from her long sleep…

Sometimes she'd poke her head out
To me

Sometimes when feeling extra brave
She'd even show her lovely face
To the world
To a dog or a cat
Maybe even another person

But she didn't trust anyone
Because all people do is hurt

Such vulnerability became at times
Almost impossible to bear

And she sometimes
Wished she'd remained in her oblivion

Immune and unaware

But the sun would shine on her body
Loving her
Warmth

The wind would whisper a song of
Encouragement in her ear

A flower would caress her nostrils
With its special scent

And slowly she began to wake from her long slumber...

She began to weep again

She began to laugh from her belly

She began to **feel**

The numbness began to dissipate
And she became flooded by sensory information
She had long forgotten or ignored

She felt the others' pain
She heard the others' head

Whose?
Mine?
Yours?

Such confusion

So she sits and sifts through the debris
That has been created by her.

That is the hardest realisation of all

There is a choice

There always was...

Fear not the future

For it is already here

Fear not the past

For it is here now

In this perfect moment of creation

Now. Forever. Never.

Is all that there is.

Rejoice!

Spirals
Circling
In my mind
Obsessive
Anger
Hurtful thoughts
Encroaching
On my consciousness
Uncertain
Where it is all heading
And what is the lesson
I face right now.

Sigh
Breathe deeply
Calm yourself
Let her stroke your hair

Do not burden
Yourself
With the journey
Of others

Sit quietly
Buddha-like
Orange robed
With golden hair
And sparkling eyes

Let the anger pass
Like a wave
Pushing
The side of the boat at sea

The sea
In her vigour and her pain
In her wisdom
And her fear

Is still the ocean.

Calm
Timeless
Deep
And true

Be free.
Be Home.

Comfortable confusion

Foggy head

Mixed with gratitude and anticipation

What is ahead is unknown

And what has happened

Means nothing

Except to allow me

To arrive at this place

And for that

I am grateful.

Relationships

Relationships suck.
Especially complicated
When sex is involved

They pick you up
Suck you in
And then spit you out
So you land
on the pavement
With an almighty thud.

You pick yourself up
Dust yourself off
You lick your wounds
You learn something from it
You reach out your hand
You start again.

Relationships.

I cling desperately to the tree branch
The river torrent, flowing too fast
Fearful that if I lose my grip
I will be lost forever…

Hoping for a miracle
Do I surrender to the river?
Or clamber my way to the shore?
Will I lose the river forever?

Your soul is at peace
But your mind tortured
Breathe
Breathe

You will not drown
Or be lost to your thoughts and fears

You have everything you need
To be happy

The river is an illusion
And so is the tree!

Just breathe
Just breathe
She whispered
Take it all in
Breathe it

This is my gift to you
For all you have given

Now may you see
As I do
How magnificent
You really are

How truly **magnificent**

And amazing

And wonderful.

                    The essence.

                              The truth.

                                        Of you.

'Be strong.
Be brave.
Stand up for yourself', she cries

'For you are nothing more
And nothing less

Than the stars and the heavens and the trees

Wake up and free yourself
From the doubts and confusion'.

I feel so utterly misunderstood right now
I know it's my fears rising
But it feels real

And I cry
Because I don't know what to do

It all seems so wrong
Each way I turn
The same
So far from the liberation
That lurks somewhere
Behind a door in my mind

I want to run away
And crawl beneath a rock

Why does this seem
Such a struggle
When everything else is effortless?

Because you fight it
You deny your truth
You couch yourself in a way
That isn't you

You protect others
Because they rise up
And bite
Like a scorpion's tail
That strikes to protect
What it knows
Simply egos.

I feel really victimised
That I don't belong

You don't need to belong
You just need to be yourself.

And you sit
And retreat
And calmly ponder

What it all means
And what it's all for

And a soft whisper
Feathers your ear

And the breeze kisses your cheek

And she strokes your hair
With her gentle touch

And you breathe

And you breathe

And you breathe.

The innocent babes frolic merrily in the sun

Two boys.
Twins.
With translucent skin of angels
And blue eyes of cherubs.

Life for them is seemingly so uncomplicated

Just joyous moment after joyous moment

Where does our innocence go as we get older?
Do we really become wiser?
Or just more cynical, fearful and afraid?

I want to experience that union of the senses again

And see life once more

Through the eyes of a child.

Woman Woman
Shining bright
In the sunshine
Of your life

Be free
To soar
Above
The pain
Of yesteryear.

Lifetimes shared
And lifetimes past

Nothing can hurt you

You're Home at last.

Just so you know: It does pass
There is light at the end of the tunnel

You return to where you began
Only changed
And everything looks a little different somehow

All you need to do
Is re-discover who you really are

And you are already that.

So often we ask why

Yet seldom do we allow the Divine

To flow through us

In its never ending journey

The rain does not ask: 'When shall I rain or how?'

It simply does as its nature decrees

Similarly the sun does not decide to shine or how

Its immeasurable light

Simply is.

So it is with us.

If we allow our nature
There is no trouble
Just peace and harmony
With the Divine within

That is our true nature

No more questions to ask

No right way to be

No place to go

Just here. Now.

As you are.

Complete
perfection.

The rainbow serpent
The fire god
The kundalini
Burning
Burning it all
Until there is nothing left
The ashes rise
Phoenix-like
To reveal a face
Of serenity

To realise
There was never a face
It just turned to see itself

Waveless ocean
Blissful sea
Total calm

Free.

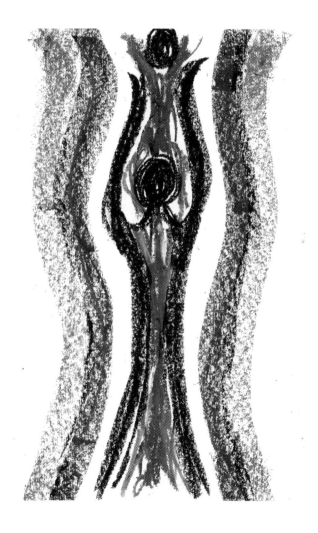

When you came to me for the first time

I felt Love

And my heart began to open...

...like a flower.

44

The eye
The eye that sees
Looks inward

The heart
The heart that's free
Beats calmly

The love
The love that flows through me

The joy
Of the hummingbird
Who sings softly
Just to please itself.

Magnificence
Knows not why it is there
Just simply that it is
And always has been
And shall continue to be

A poet
A lover
A wife
A dreamer
An idealist
A slave
A child
A mother
A hoper
A screamer
A salvation

A vision of what is to come
A dreamer of all things
A knower of all truths
A believer in all things real
And tangible

And godlike
And phoenix-like
Liberated
Home
Home
Home at last she cries

I will never leave this place
I will never forget again

Freedom sings and cries and roars

And a tear is shed.

The mind is like an onion
Layer upon layer
Life's experiences
Add another level

That when removed
Can make you cry
For the pain of it
the joy of it
The sheer liberation of relief

And what do we find at the core of it?

No-thing-ness.

Blissful, sweet, true.

I meditated
I masturbated
I cogitated
I copulated
I loved
I hated
I cried
I laughed
I wondered when
I'd be Home at last

Confusion
Doubt
Elation
Joy
Sorrow
Pity
I wonder why?

What makes some
Seemingly
So stable
So sure

When I was living in my own private hell?

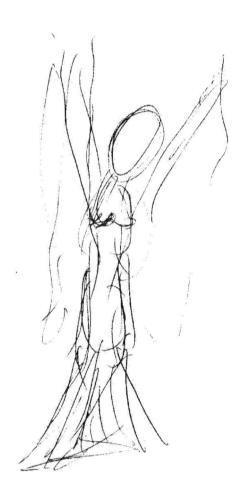

Living beyond the ego

Is about not needing to say how good you are -
Just knowing it inside

About doing it for love,
Not recognition

About not judging yourself as better than someone else
Because comparisons with others don't exist

It's about being kind to yourself
And not pressuring yourself with promises you cannot keep

It's about integration, not struggle

It's often elusive,
but seeking it is a gift and a challenge

It's about unconditional love
And connectedness with the universe in its entirety

It's about living in your heart and not in your head.

Enlightenment is merely the beginning of the journey.

We must then work out how it is we can best
help others remember who they are.

For in becoming lost, we have simply
forgotten who we are.

The process is never ending and to perceive that
an end point exists is to miss the point.

There is no end or beginning.

Such concepts are an illusion and serve
to elude us from the Truth.

Created by the ego who cleverly deceives us.

For to live our Truth threatens its existence.
It no longer has a place.

Oh what sweet liberation!

Make no mistake:
You are not the waves in the ocean
But the ocean itself.

The stillness of the
Vast
Calm
Timeless
Ocean.

That
Is who you are.

Remember this:

You are your own **truest** friend

Most **tender** lover

And wisest **sage**.

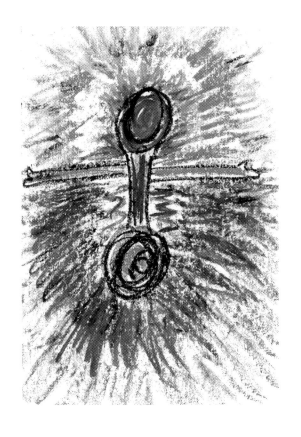

When we realise that we are the universe,

there is no place for concepts,

and all mountainous burdens disappear.

We are already free!

'What do you want from me?' I asked.

And he said: 'All I want to know is: can you give me tenderness?'

And in that moment, it was the only thing I knew I had for sure in abundance.

She wears her pain with a smile
Taking her moments when she needs to
And embracing the healing

She lets you know her
In a way that works for you
Kindly, gently, nurturing
With few words
But with a heart
A presence
A love

That fills to overflowing and beyond
Into the boundary-less abyss
Of Bliss.

Carved by pain
So deep
To hold it in one heart
Seems impossible

So she lets it out
A little at a time

Tells her story
And in so telling
And retelling
And refining
And re-defining
And re–conceptualising
And remembering

She changes the space
it takes away

So there is more room

For the things she
wants there

And in a funny sort of way
(she knows that better than me)
When you see something
That's held you back

It suddenly has no power over you
Anymore

And you can feel its cold, spiky fingers
Loosen
Then lose their grip

And the eagle can stretch her wings
Wider than before
Stronger than before

Phoenix-like

Free

Free at last
She knows
Knows deep within
That she is free
Truly free

For the first time

Again.

Big brown eyes

Looking up at me

Confidently

Wisely

Hopefully

Unflinchingly

Seeing into me

Waiting

Patiently

Hopefully

Expectantly

Smiling at me

Warmly

Innocently

Truthfully

Openly

Begging me

Desperately

Silently

Eagerly

Knowingly.

Sharing our humanity.

She dances

She smiles

She sings

She shines

She teaches

She nurtures

She graces

She embraces

She blossoms

She expresses

She radiates

She plays

She is completely herself in this moment

Authentic

Loving

Graceful

True.

Just watch your breath
For a moment

And all balance and peace
Will be restored.

How can I feel
I want to share all of me
With you
And yet know
It would just make
our lives
more complicated
than they need to be?

So I must walk away
Knowing it will be
Exactly the same the next time we meet...
And the time after that...

What a strange, beautiful
And enduring love and friendship we share.
How fortunate we are.

I've always been scared

To let go

In case I fell

Into the deep, dark abyss

And never returned

But the other day

A funny thing happened

I realised

That if I let go

I might be lifted up

As if to soar on eagle's wings.

Oh what sweet liberation that was!

Before you
I stand naked
In my vulnerability
In my truth
Where we meet
In love
To understand and forgive and heal

For in me
You have another
Who sees you
As you are

Perfect. Whole. Complete.

me

you

Let's just pretend, OK?

You can come and sit in my garden

I will make you coffee
And I'll have tea

And we can just, you know,

Be.

Small steps

She takes her first step

Gingerly

Shyly

Uncertainly

She looks around

                    She is safe

She takes another

Cautiously

Nervously

Hopefully

She is safe

Again, she bravely moves forth
Unknowingly
Wantingly
Expectantly

The sun peaks from behind its cloud

And she smiles
To herself

She peers around
there is nothing to fear

She claps her hands
With delight

She boldly strides forth

Her head held high

Fearless

Courageous

Strong

To her destination

She followed
She was led
She let go
She grew strong
She faced her fears

Shamanistic transformation

Then watched the layers of
Her pain
Mercifully unfold
Sometimes painfully
Always liberating
Surrender in each moment
Holding onto the hope
The whisper
The promise
Of who she is
And all she can be
In each moment
Each step easier
Until she returns
To the place she began
And realises the movement
Was internal
And faith her guide

That drove her forth
When blindly she knew
Not where it led

Simply that she must

Now she flies above the sky
With her face to the sun

And her heart

The ocean.

Evolution...

We are all petals
Of the Divine

With our own unique
Story, voice and message

Radiant

Blossoming

Perfect

You.